5 MINUTE MEALS

QUICK AND EASY RECIPES FOR BUSY FAMILIES

CW01619419

Copyright

5 MINUTE MEALS

QUICK AND EASY RECIPES FOR BUSY FAMILIES

BETHANY FOX

DISCLAIMER

GENERAL SAFETY DISCLAIMER

The reader must take the responsibility to review the listed ingredients before cooking to ensure none of the ingredients causes potential adverse effects to anyone consuming the food. Adverse effects include allergies, issues arising due to health-related restricted diet, and pregnancy-related effects.

KIDS COOKING SAFETY DISCLAIMER

Cooking with kids is fun and equally messy but it is a great bonding time and creates memorable moments. However, child safety measures should be given the highest priority. Readers must take utmost safety measures when handling the kids in the kitchen. It is the reader's responsibility to supervise and assist the child all the time and ensure all the necessary protection measures are taken and appropriate clothing is provided. Always monitor the child while handling electrical appliances.

Although there is no definite age to introduce kids to kitchen tasks, the reader as a parent/guardian should take responsibility for judging the child's capabilities and assign tasks accordingly. Do not allow small children to handle electrical appliances or sharp objects such as knives. Take extra care when kids are near hot surfaces and hot equipment.

PREP TIME AND COOK TIME DISCLAIMER

I try my best to estimate accurate prep and cooking time for recipes, however, it might differ from person to person. I take less than half a minute to finely chop an onion, whereas my husband takes more than a minute!

TABLE OF CONTENTS

TABLE OF CONTENTS

Introduction

Are you a busy parent struggling to balance work, household chores, and quality time with your family? Do you feel like you're always running out of time and repeatedly feeding your kids the same thing? If so, you're not alone. I know all too well how hard it is to find time, energy, and inspiration to cook healthy family meals that your kids will eat and that can be on the table in minutes. Many families today face the same challenges, and it's often difficult to resist the temptation of fast food or a microwave-ready meal. But there is another way!

In my book Time Management for Families (available at Amazon), I researched cooking using time-saving equipment such as a slow cooker. When you get savvy with kitchen gadgets, you open yourself up to a whole new world of cooking in minutes.

In this book, I have advised cooking using time-efficient kitchen equipment for some recipes. However, you can make all the recipes with the equipment you already have in the kitchen: instead of a soup maker, you can use a pan on the hob; instead of the slow cooker or microwave, you can use the oven - it just might take you a little longer. If you have the equipment advised, you only need to spend five minutes preparing in the kitchen to create these recipes.

What's more, anyone in the family can cook all these recipes, and I very much encourage you to cook with your kids. Cooking with your children is an excellent way to bond and engage with them and for them to learn vital life skills at the same time. From vibrant salads and nourishing soups to hearty mains and indulgent desserts, these recipes prioritize simplicity without sacrificing the richness of flavor. With just a handful of readily available ingredients and straightforward instructions, you'll be amazed at how effortlessly you can whip up a fantastic meal in mere minutes.

So, dust off your apron, get your kids on board, and prepare to embark on a culinary adventure that will revolutionize your kitchen. With these 5-minute meals, you'll unlock a world of convenience, flavor, and quality time spent with your loved ones. Embrace the joy of quick and easy cooking and savor the delightful rewards it brings to your family's table.

Please consider leaving me a review for this book on Amazon and let me know what you think about the recipes. Feedback is so important to me so I can evaluate my work and hopefully bring you exciting new books in the future.

Bethany

SLOW COOKER RECIPES

HONEY GARLIC CHICKEN

Prep time
5 Min

Cook Time
4 Hour

Servings
4

Ingredients

- 4 boneless, skinless chicken breasts
- 1/2 cup honey
- 1/2 cup low-sodium soy sauce
- 4 cloves garlic, minced
- 1/4 cup ketchup
- Small pack of sliced mushrooms
- 1 tsp dried oregano

Directions

1. Put the chicken breasts and mushrooms in your slow cooker.
2. Mix honey, soy sauce, garlic, ketchup, and oregano in a small bowl.
3. Pour the mixture over the chicken.
4. Cook for 4 hours on low with the lid on the slow cooker.
5. Serve with crusty bread or microwaved rice and garnish with chopped parsley if desired.

JACKET POTATOES WITH BEANS & CHEESE

Prep time
5 Min

Cook Time
6-8 Hour

Servings
4

Ingredients

- 4 large russet potatoes, cleaned
- 1 can (15 oz) baked beans
- 1 cup shredded cheese (cheddar, mozzarella, or your choice)
- Salt and pepper, to taste

Directions

1. Wash and dry the potatoes. Prick them a few times with a fork.
2. Place the potatoes in the slow cooker without any liquid or foil.
3. Cook on LOW for 6-8 hours until potatoes are tender.
4. Cut a slit across the top of each potato and gently fluff the insides.
5. Season with salt and pepper.
6. Fill each potato with beans and sprinkle cheese on top.
7. Put the lid back on and cook for another 15 minutes until cheese melts.
8. Serve the slow cooker jacket potatoes with beans and cheese.

SLOW COOKER BEEF STEW WITH ROOT VEGETABLES

Prep time
8 Min

Cook Time
8 Hour

Servings
6

Ingredients

- 2 lbs beef stew meat, cut into bite-sized pieces
- 4 carrots, peeled and chopped
- 3 potatoes, peeled and cubed
- 1 onion, diced
- 2 cloves garlic, minced
- 1 cup beef broth
- 1 cup red wine (optional)
- 2 tablespoons tomato paste
- 2 teaspoons dried thyme
- 2 teaspoons dried rosemary
- Salt and pepper to taste
- 2 tablespoons all-purpose flour (optional, for thickening)
- Fresh parsley, chopped (for garnish)

Directions

1. In a large slow cooker, combine the beef stew meat, carrots, potatoes, onion, and garlic.
2. In a separate bowl, whisk together the beef broth, red wine (if using), tomato paste, thyme, rosemary, salt, and pepper. Pour the mixture over the ingredients in the slow cooker.
3. Stir everything together to ensure the meat and vegetables are coated with the liquid.
4. Cover the slow cooker and prepare on low for 8 hours, or until the beef is tender and the flavors have melded together.
5. If desired, to thicken the stew, mix the flour with a little water to make a slurry. Stir the slurry into the slow cooker during the last 30 minutes of cooking.
6. Once cooked, taste and adjust the seasoning if needed.
7. Serve the Slow Cooker Beef Stew with Root Vegetables hot, garnished with fresh parsley. It pairs well with crusty bread or rice for a satisfying and comforting meal. Enjoy!

VEGETARIAN CHILLI

Prep time
5 Min

Cook Time
4 Hour

Servings
6

Ingredients

- 1 can kidney beans, drained and rinsed
- 1 can black beans, drained and rinsed
- 1 can corn, drained
- 1 can dice tomatoes with green chillis
- 1 onion, chopped
- 1 bell pepper, chopped
- 1 packet of chilli seasoning

Directions

1. Add beans, corn, diced tomatoes, green chillis, onion, bell pepper, and chilli seasoning to your slow cooker.
2. Mix well to combine all the ingredients.
3. Cover the slow cooker and set it on low for 4 hours.
4. After the cooking time, stir the chilli well and serve hot. You can garnish it with shredded cheese, sour cream, or chopped green onions for an added layer of flavor.

CHICKEN AND WILD RICE SOUP

Prep time
5 Min

Cook Time
6 Hour

Servings
6

Ingredients

- 2 boneless, skinless chicken breasts
- 1 cup uncooked wild rice
- 1 onion, chopped
- 2 carrots, chopped
- 2 stalks of celery, chopped
- 4 cups chicken broth
- 1 tsp dried thyme
- Salt and pepper to taste

Directions

1. Place chicken breasts, wild rice, onion, carrots, celery, chicken broth, thyme, salt, and pepper in your slow cooker.
2. Stir well to ensure everything is well combined.
3. Cover and cook on low for 6 hours.
4. Before serving, with two forks, shred the chicken breasts and mix them well into the soup.
5. Serve with crusty bread if desired.

CHICKEN FAJITAS

Prep time
5 Min

Cook Time
4 Hour

Servings
6

Ingredients

- 3 boneless, skinless chicken breasts
- 1 onion, sliced
- 2 bell peppers, sliced
- 1 packet of fajita seasoning
- 1/4 cup water

Directions

1. Set the chicken in the bottom of your slow cooker.
2. Sprinkle the fajita seasoning over the chicken.
3. Top with sliced onions and bell peppers.
4. Add water and cover the slow cooker.
5. Cook on low for 4 hours.
6. Shred the chicken and serve with warm tortillas and your favorite fajita toppings.

BEEF AND BROCCOLI

Prep time
5 Min

Cook Time
4 Hour

Servings
4

Ingredients

- 1 lb beef stew meat
- 1 cup beef broth
- 1/2 cup soy sauce
- 1/4 cup brown sugar
- 2 cloves garlic, minced
- 2 tbsp cornstarch
- 2 heads of broccoli, cut into florets

Directions

1. Add beef, broth, soy sauce, brown sugar, and minced garlic to your slow cooker.
2. Stir well to combine.
3. Cover and cook on low for 4 hours.
4. Thirty minutes before serving, whisk together cornstarch with 2 tbsp of cold water in a small-size bowl.
5. Stir the cornstarch mixture and broccoli florets into the slow cooker.
6. Cover and cook for another 30 mins until the sauce has thickened and the broccoli is tender. Serve with cooked rice, noodles or crusty bread.

PULLED PORK SANDWICHES

Prep time
5 Min

Cook Time
8 Hour

Servings
6

Ingredients

- 2 lbs pork shoulder
- 1 cup BBQ sauce
- 1/2 cup apple cider vinegar
- 1/2 cup chicken broth
- 1/2 cup brown sugar
- 1 tbsp mustard
- 1 tbsp Worcestershire sauce
- 1 onion, chopped
- 2 cloves garlic, minced

Directions

1. Set the pork shoulder into the slow cooker.
2. Mix BBQ sauce, apple cider vinegar, chicken broth, brown sugar, mustard, Worcestershire sauce, chopped onion, and minced garlic in a bowl.
3. Pour the mixture over the pork shoulder.
4. Cover and cook on low for 8 hours or until the pork is soft and easy to shred.
5. Shred the pork and thoroughly combine it with the sauce using two forks. If desired, serve on buns with coleslaw.

STUFFED BELL PEPPERS

Prep time
5 Min

Cook Time
6 Hour

Servings
4

Ingredients

- 4 bell peppers
- 1 lb ground beef
- 1 cup cooked rice
- 1 can diced tomatoes
- 1 onion, chopped
- 2 cloves garlic, minced
- 1 cup shredded cheese
- Salt and pepper to taste

Directions

1. Cut the tops off the bell peppers, then remove the seeds and membranes.
2. Mix ground beef, cooked rice, diced tomatoes, chopped onion, minced garlic, half the cheese, salt, and pepper in a bowl.
3. Stuff the peppers with the mixture and place them into the slow cooker.
4. Cook on low, covering with a lid for 6 hours.
5. Sprinkle the remaining cheese over the peppers, cover again, and cook until the cheese melts. Serve hot.

SALSA CHICKEN

Prep time
5 Min

Cook Time
4 Hour

Servings
4

Ingredients

- 4 boneless, skinless chicken breasts
- 1 jar salsa
- 1 packet of taco seasoning
- 1 can black beans, drained and rinsed
- 1 can corn, drained

Directions

1. Set chicken breasts at the bottom of the slow cooker.
2. Sprinkle taco seasoning over the chicken.
3. Pour over salsa, then add black beans and corn.
4. Cover and cook on low for 4 hours.
5. In the pot, shred the chicken and stir to combine well with the salsa mixture.
6. Serve with warmed tortillas.

BEEF STROGANOFF

Prep time
5 Min

Cook Time
6 Hour

Servings
4

Ingredients

- 1 lb beef stew meat
- 1 onion, chopped
- 2 cloves garlic, minced
- 1 cup beef broth
- 1 small pack of mushrooms
- 1 cup sour cream
- 1 can condensed mushroom soup
- Salt and pepper to taste

Directions

1. Combine beef, mushrooms, onion, garlic, broth, and condensed mushroom soup in your slow cooker.
2. Cover and prepare on low for 6 hours.
3. Stir in the sour cream and then season with salt and pepper. Continue to cook on low for another 15 minutes until heated through.
4. Serve over cooked egg noodles or microwaved rice with a sprinkle of fresh parsley.

SWEET AND SOUR CHICKEN

Prep time
5 Min

Cook Time
4 Hour

Servings
4

Ingredients

- 4 boneless, skinless chicken breasts
- 1 can pineapple chunks, drained with juice reserved
- 1 bell pepper, chopped
- 1/2 cup ketchup
- 1/3 cup brown sugar
- 1/4 cup vinegar
- 2 tbsp cornstarch
- Salt and pepper to taste

Directions

1. Place chicken breasts into the slow cooker.
2. Whisk the pineapple juice, ketchup, brown sugar, vinegar, and cornstarch in a bowl. Pour the mixture over the chicken.
3. Top with drained pineapple chunks and chopped bell pepper.
4. Cover and cook on low for 4 hours.
5. Shred the chicken in the pot and then stir to combine well with the sauce. Season with salt and pepper. Serve over cooked rice or with crusty bread.

LEMON GARLIC CHICKEN

Prep time
5 Min

Cook Time
4 Hour

Servings
4

Ingredients

- 4 boneless, skinless chicken breasts
- 3 cloves garlic, minced
- 1/4 cup lemon juice
- 1 tsp dried rosemary
- Salt and pepper to taste
- 1 lemon, sliced

Directions

1. Set the chicken breasts into the slow cooker.
2. Mix minced garlic, lemon juice, dried rosemary, salt, and pepper in a small bowl. Pour this mixture over the chicken.
3. Top with lemon slices.
4. Cover and prepare on low for 4 hours.
5. Serve the chicken with the delicious lemon garlic sauce spooned over the top and a green salad.

CRANBERRY TURKEY BREAST

Prep time
5 Min

Cook Time
4-6 Min

Servings
6

Ingredients

- 3-4 pounds boneless turkey breast
- 1 cup cranberry sauce
- 1/4 cup orange juice
- 2 tablespoons honey
- 2 tablespoons Dijon mustard
- 1 teaspoon dried rosemary
- 1/2 teaspoon dried thyme
- 1/2 teaspoon salt
- 1/4 teaspoon black pepper
- Fresh cranberries and rosemary sprigs (for garnish)

Directions

1. Place the boneless turkey breast in the slow cooker.
2. In a bowl, mix together the cranberry sauce, orange juice, honey, Dijon mustard, dried rosemary, dried thyme, salt, and black pepper.
3. Pour the cranberry mixture over the turkey breast in the slow cooker, making sure it is well coated.
4. Cover the slow cooker and cook on low for 4-6 hours until the turkey is cooked through and reaches an internal temperature of 165°F (75°C).
5. Once cooked, carefully remove the turkey breast from the slow cooker and let it rest for a few minutes.
6. Slice the turkey and transfer it to a serving platter.
7. Spoon some of the cranberry sauce mixture from the slow cooker over the sliced turkey.
8. Garnish with fresh cranberries and rosemary sprigs for an elegant presentation.
9. Serve the Cranberry Turkey Breast with a fresh green salad.

BEEF TACOS

Prep time
5 Min

Cook Time
8 Hour

Servings
6

Ingredients

- 2 lbs beef chuck roast
- 1 packet of taco seasoning
- 1 cup beef broth
- 1 onion, chopped
- 2 cloves garlic, minced
- Taco shells and toppings for serving

Directions

1. Sprinkle the beef chuck roast with the taco seasoning, then place it into the slow cooker.
2. Add the chopped onion, minced garlic, and beef broth.
3. Cover and prepare on low for 8 hours.
4. Shred the beef in your slow cooker with two forks.
5. Serve the shredded beef in taco shells with your favorite taco toppings.

VEGGIE LASAGNA

Prep time
5 Min

Cook Time
4 Hour

Servings
6

Ingredients

- 2 cups ricotta cheese
- 1 cup grated Parmesan cheese
- 2 cups shredded mozzarella cheese
- 1 jar marinara sauce
- 2 zucchinis, sliced
- 1 bell pepper, chopped
- No-boil lasagna noodles

Directions

1. Mix the ricotta, Parmesan, and half of the mozzarella cheese in a bowl.
2. Spread a layer of marinara sauce at the bottom of the slow cooker.
3. Layer on top: uncooked lasagna noodles (breaking to fit as necessary), a portion of the cheese mixture, zucchini slices, and bell pepper.
4. Repeat the layers until the ingredients are used up, finishing with a layer of marinara sauce.
5. Cover and cook on low for 4 hours.
6. Sprinkle the remaining mozzarella on top, cover again, and let it melt before serving.

CREAMY GARLIC CHICKEN

Prep time
5 Min

Cook Time
4 Hour

Servings
4

Ingredients

- 4 boneless, skinless chicken breasts
- 2 cups cream of chicken soup
- 3 cloves of garlic, minced
- Handful of baby corn
- 1 zucchini
- Small pack of mushrooms
- Salt and pepper to taste
- Parsley for garnish

Directions

1. Put the chicken breasts and vegetables into the slow cooker.
2. Mix the cream of chicken soup, minced garlic, salt, and pepper in a bowl.
3. Pour the soup mixture over the chicken.
4. Cover and cook on low for 4 hours. Stir occasionally.
5. Serve the creamy garlic chicken garnished with chopped parsley and fresh bread.

CHILLI BEEF

Prep time
5 Min

Cook Time
8 Hour

Servings
6

Ingredients

- 1 lb ground beef
- 1 onion, chopped
- 2 cloves garlic, minced
- 1 can of kidney beans, drained
- 1 can diced tomatoes
- 1 zucchini sliced
- 1 eggplant diced
- 1 carrot diced
- 1 pack of button mushrooms
- 2 tbsp chilli powder
- Salt and pepper to taste

Directions

1. Place all the ingredients in the slow cooker.
2. Stir until well mixed.
3. Cover and cook on low for 8 hours.
4. If you want, serve with a dollop of sour cream and chopped cheese.

CREAMY TOMATO BASIL PASTA

Prep time
5 Min

Cook Time
4-6 Hour

Servings
4

Ingredients

- 8 oz pasta of your choice
- 1 can (14 oz) diced tomatoes
- 1 cup tomato sauce
- 1/2 cup heavy cream
- 2 cloves garlic, minced
- 1 teaspoon dried basil
- 1/2 teaspoon dried oregano
- 1/2 teaspoon salt
- 1/4 teaspoon black pepper
- Fresh basil leaves, chopped (for garnish)

Directions

1. In the slow cooker, combine diced tomatoes, tomato sauce, heavy cream, minced garlic, dried basil, dried oregano, salt, and black pepper.
2. Stir the ingredients together until well combined.
3. Add the uncooked pasta to the slow cooker, making sure it is submerged in the sauce.
4. Cover the slow cooker and cook on low for 4-6 hours or until the pasta is tender.
5. Stir the pasta occasionally during cooking to prevent sticking.
6. Once cooked, garnish with fresh basil leaves.
7. Serve the creamy tomato basil pasta hot and enjoy!

SLOW-COOKER CREAMED CORN

Prep time
5 Min

Cook Time
4 Hour

Servings
6

Ingredients

- 6 cups fresh or frozen corn kernels
- 8 oz cream cheese, softened
- 1/2 cup unsalted butter
- 1/2 cup milk
- 2 tablespoons granulated sugar
- 1 teaspoon salt
- 1/2 teaspoon black pepper
- Chopped fresh parsley for garnish

Directions

1. Place the corn kernels, cream cheese, butter, milk, sugar, salt, and black pepper in the slow cooker.
2. Stir well to combine all the ingredients.
3. Cover and cook on low for 4 hours, stirring occasionally.
4. The creamed corn is ready once the corn is tender and the cream cheese and butter have melted completely.
5. Taste and adjust the seasoning if needed.
6. Serve the slow-cooker creamed corn hot with crusty bread, garnished with chopped fresh parsley.

LAMB WITH PISTACHIO AND POMEGRANATE

Prep time
5 Min

Cook Time
6 Hour

Servings
4

Ingredients

- 2 lbs lamb shoulder, cut into chunks
- 1 onion, chopped
- 1 zucchini roughly chopped
- 1 eggplant diced
- 3 cloves of garlic, minced
- Salt and pepper to taste
- 1 cup beef broth
- 1/4 cup pomegranate molasses
- 1/2 cup pistachios, shelled and roughly chopped
- Seeds of 1 pomegranate for garnish

Directions

1. Salt and pepper the meat chunks and put them in the slow cooker.
2. Add the chopped onion and minced garlic.
3. Pour in the beef broth and pomegranate molasses.
4. Cover and cook on low for 6 hours.
5. Before serving, stir in the chopped pistachios.
6. Serve the lamb garnished with pomegranate seeds.

SWEDISH MEATBALLS

Prep time
5 Min

Cook Time
6 Hour

Servings
6

Ingredients

- 2 lbs frozen meatballs
- 1 can cream of mushroom soup
- 1 packet dry onion soup mix
- 1 cup beef broth
- 1 cup sour cream
- Salt and pepper to taste
- Chopped parsley for garnish

Directions

1. In the slow cooker, place the frozen meatballs.
2. Mix the cream of mushroom soup, dry onion soup, and beef broth in a bowl.
3. Pour the soup mixture over the meatballs.
4. Cover and cook on low for 6 hours.
5. Before serving, stir in the sour cream. Season with salt and pepper to taste.
6. Serve the Swedish meatballs in a sub roll garnished with chopped parsley

KUNG PAO CHICKEN NOODLES

Prep time
5 Min

Cook Time
4 Hour

Servings
4

Ingredients

- 4 boneless, skinless breasts of chicken cut into chunks
- 1/4 cup soy sauce
- 1/4 cup hoisin sauce
- 2 tablespoons rice vinegar
- 1 teaspoon sesame oil
- 2 garlic cloves, minced
- 1 tablespoon grated ginger
- 1/2 teaspoon red pepper flakes
- 1/2 cup unsalted dry roasted peanuts
- 1/4 cup water
- 8 oz cooked egg noodles
- Sliced green onions and additional peanuts for garnish

Directions

1. Combine chicken, soy sauce, hoisin sauce, rice vinegar, sesame oil, garlic, ginger, red pepper flakes, and peanuts in your slow cooker.
2. Cover with a lid and cook on low for 4 hours.
3. Serve the Kung Pao Chicken over cooked egg noodles, then garnish with sliced green onions and additional peanuts.

SLOW COOKER CHICKEN WINGS

Prep time
5 Min

Cook Time
3 Hour

Servings
4

Ingredients

- 2 lbs chicken wings
- 1 cup BBQ sauce
- 1/4 cup honey
- 2 cloves garlic, minced
- Salt and pepper to taste
- Chopped parsley for garnish

Directions

1. Using salt and pepper to season the chicken wings and place them into the slow cooker.
2. Mix the BBQ sauce, honey, and minced garlic in a bowl.
3. Pour the sauce over the chicken wings, ensuring they are coated well.
4. Cover and cook on low for 3 hours.
5. After 3 hours, you can choose to serve them as is, or for a crispy finish, place the wings on a baking tray and broil for 2-3 minutes in the oven.
6. Serve the chicken wings garnished with chopped parsley and green salad.

QUICK AND EASY LAMB CURRY

Prep time
5 Min

Cook Time
4-6 Min

Servings
4

Ingredients

- 1.5 lbs boneless lamb, cut into chunks
- 2 tablespoons curry powder
- 1 onion, chopped
- 3 cloves garlic, minced
- 1 can (14 oz) diced tomatoes
- 1 cup chicken broth
- Salt and pepper to taste
- Fresh cilantro leaves, for garnish

Directions

1. In a slow cooker, combine the lamb chunks, curry powder, chopped onion, minced garlic, diced tomatoes (with their juices), and chicken broth.
2. Season with salt and pepper to taste.
3. Stir the ingredients together until well combined.
4. Cover the slow cooker and cook on low for 4-6 hours or until the lamb is tender and cooked through.
5. Once cooked, garnish with fresh cilantro leaves.
6. Serve the lamb curry hot with steamed rice or naan bread.

BRAISED DUCK WITH SHALLOTS, PORCINI, AND COUSCOUS

Prep time
5 Min

Cook Time
4 Hour

Servings
4

Ingredients

- 2 duck breasts
- 8 shallots, peeled and halved
- 1 cup dried porcini mushrooms
- 1 cup chicken broth
- 1 cup red wine
- Salt and pepper to taste
- 1 cup couscous
- 2 cups water

Directions

1. Season the duck breasts with salt & pepper, then place them in the slow cooker.
2. Add the shallots and dried porcini mushrooms.
3. Add in the chicken broth and red wine.
4. Cover and cook on low for 4 hours.
5. Five minutes before serving, cover the couscous with boiling water and a pan lid.
6. To serve, plate the couscous and top with the slow-cooked duck, shallots, and porcini. Drizzle some of the cooking liquid over the top for extra flavor.

MOROCCAN LAMB TAGINE

Prep time
5 Min

Cook Time
6 Hour

Servings
4

Ingredients

- 2 lbs lamb shoulder, cut into chunks
- 2 teaspoons Moroccan spice mix (ras el hanout)
- 1 onion, chopped
- 1 zucchini sliced
- 2 cloves garlic, minced
- 1 can chickpeas, drained and rinsed
- 1 cup dried apricots
- 2 cups chicken broth
- Salt and pepper to taste
- Fresh mint and couscous to serve

Directions

1. Combine all the ingredients except the couscous and mint in the slow cooker.
2. Cover and cook on low for 6 hours.
3. Just before serving, prepare couscous according to packet instructions.
4. Serve the Moroccan Lamb Tagine over couscous, garnished with fresh mint.

HAWAIIAN PINEAPPLE CHICKEN

Prep time
5 Min

Cook Time
4 Hour

Servings
4

Ingredients

- 4 boneless, skinless chicken breasts
- 1 can pineapple chunks with juice
- 1/4 cup soy sauce
- 1/4 cup brown sugar
- 1 bell pepper, chopped
- 2 cups cooked rice to serve
- Sliced green onions for garnish

Directions

1. Combine the chicken breasts, pineapple chunks with juice, soy sauce, brown sugar, and chopped bell pepper in your slow cooker.
2. Cover and cook in the cooker on low for 4 hours.
3. Serve the Hawaiian Pineapple Chicken over cooked rice, garnished with sliced green onions.

SLOW COOKER CARNITAS

Prep time
5 Min

Cook Time
6 Hour

Servings
6

Ingredients

- 2 lbs pork shoulder
- 2 teaspoons salt
- 1 teaspoon black pepper
- 1 tablespoon oregano
- 1 tablespoon cumin
- 2 onions, chopped
- 4 cloves garlic, minced
- 2 oranges, juiced
- Corn tortillas to serve
- Fresh cilantro and lime wedges for garnish

Directions

1. Season the pork shoulder with salt, pepper, oregano and cumin and place in the slow cooker.
2. Add the chopped onions and minced garlic.
3. Squeeze the juice of two oranges over the ingredients in the slow cooker.
4. Cover and cook in your cooker on low for 6 hours.
5. Once done, shred the pork with two forks. Optionally crisp up the shredded pork under a broiler for 2-3 minutes.
6. Serve the Carnitas on corn tortillas, garnished with fresh cilantro and lime wedges.

SHRIMP AND CRAB BISQUE

Prep time
5 Min

Cook Time
4 Hour

Servings
4-6

Ingredients

- 1 lb shrimp, peeled and deveined
- 1 cup lump crab meat
- 1 onion, diced
- 2 cloves garlic, minced
- 1 can diced tomatoes
- 4 cups seafood or vegetable broth
- 1 cup heavy cream
- Salt and pepper to taste
- Fresh dill for garnish

Directions

1. Add your peeled, deveined shrimp and lump crab meat to the slow cooker.
2. Follow with the diced onion and minced garlic.
3. Proceed to pour in the can of diced tomatoes, including the juice.
4. Add your chosen broth next; either seafood or vegetable will work.
5. Cover with a lid the slow cooker and allow it to cook on a low setting for 4 hours.
6. Once the cooking time has passed, stir in your heavy cream.
7. Taste and then adjust the seasoning with salt & pepper as necessary.
8. Ladle the Shrimp and Crab Bisque into bowls and garnish with a sprinkling of fresh dill before serving with crusty bread.

SPEEDY DESSERTS AND SOUPS

5-MINUTE MUG BROWNIE

Prep time
2 Min

Cook Time
2 Min

Servings
1

Ingredients

- 4 tablespoons flour
- 4 tablespoons sugar
- 2 tablespoons cocoa powder
- 2 tablespoons vegetable oil
- 2 tablespoons water
- Pinch of salt

Directions

1. Mix the flour, sugar, cocoa powder & salt in a microwave-safe mug.
2. Add the vegetable oil and water. Stir until there are no lumps.
3. Prepare in the microwave for 90 seconds to 2 minutes or until the center of the brownies is set, depending on their size. Let it cool for a minute before digging in.

INSTANT BANANA ICE CREAM

Prep time
5 Min

Cook Time
0 Min

Servings
2

Ingredients

- 2 ripe bananas frozen
- 1/4 cup milk of choice

Directions

1. Cut the frozen bananas into slices.
2. Put the sliced bananas in a food processor or powerful blender. Blend until smooth, adding milk as needed.
3. Serve right away or store in the freezer in an airtight container.

QUICK STRAWBERRY PARFAIT

Prep time
5 Min

Cook Time
0 Min

Servings
1

Ingredients

- 1 cup Greek yogurt
- 1/2 cup granola
- 1/2 cup fresh strawberries, chopped
- Honey to taste

Directions

1. In a glass or jar, layer 1/3 of the Greek yogurt, followed by 1/3 of the granola & 1/3 of the strawberries. Repeat layers twice more.
2. Drizzle with honey to taste.

EASY PEACH COBBLER

Prep time
2 Min

Cook Time
2 Min

Servings
4

Ingredients

- 1 can of peach slices, drained
- 1 cup granola
- 1/4 cup brown sugar
- Whipped cream or ice cream (optional)

Directions

1. Divide the peach slices between 4 microwave-safe mugs.
2. Top each mug with 1/4 cup of granola and a tablespoon of brown sugar.
3. Microwave each mug for 1-2 minutes until the brown sugar is melted. Let cool for a minute before serving.

INSTANT FRUIT SORBET

Prep time
5 Min

Cook Time
0 Min

Servings
2

Ingredients

- 2 cups frozen fruit of choice
- 1/4 cup sugar or sweetener of desire
- 1/4 cup water

Directions

1. Blend the frozen fruit, sugar, and water until smooth in a blender or food processor.
2. Serve right away or store in the freezer in an airtight container.

NO-BAKE ENERGY BALLS

Prep time
5 Min

Cook Time
0 Min

Servings
10 Balls

Ingredients

- 1 cup old-fashioned oats
- 1/2 cup peanut butter
- 1/2 cup chocolate chips
- 1/3 cup honey
- 1 teaspoon vanilla extract

Directions

1. Mix all the ingredients in a large-size bowl until well combined.
2. Using your hands, form them into balls. Place them on a sheet of parchment paper in a baking dish.
3. Chill in the freezer for at least an hour before serving.

GREEK YOGURT WITH HONEY AND NUTS

Prep time
5 Min

Cook Time
0 Min

Servings
1

Ingredients

- 1 cup Greek yogurt
- 1 tablespoon honey
- 1/4 cup mixed nuts (like almonds, walnuts & pistachios)

Directions

1. Spoon the Greek yogurt into a bowl.
2. Drizzle with honey and top with the mixed nuts.

CHOCOLATE DIPPED STRAWBERRIES

Prep time
3 Min

Cook Time
2 Min

Servings
2

Ingredients

- 1/2 cup chocolate chips
- 10 strawberries

Directions

1. Melt the chocolate chips in the bowl that can go in the microwave for 30 seconds, stirring after each 30 seconds.
2. Once the chocolate is smooth, dip each strawberry in the chocolate. Set them on a plate placed with parchment paper.
3. Chill in the refrigerator until the chocolate is set.

MICROWAVE RICE KRISPIE TREAT

Prep time	Cook Time	Servings
2 Min	2 Min	4

Ingredients

- 2 cups Rice Krispies cereal
- 1 cup marshmallows
- 1 tablespoon butter

Directions

1. In a microwave-safe bowl, mix the marshmallows and butter. Microwave for 1 min or until the marshmallows are puffy.
2. Remove from the microwave and stir until the butter and marshmallows are well combined.
3. Stir in the Rice Krispies cereal until it gets evenly coated.
4. Press the mixture into a greased dish or onto a plate. Let it cool before cutting it into squares.

5-MINUTE CHEESECAKE IN A MUG

Prep time
2 Min

Cook Time
2 Min

Servings
1

Ingredients

- 1/4 cup cream cheese
- 1/4 cup Greek yogurt
- 2 tablespoons sugar
- 1/4 teaspoon vanilla extract
- 1/2 egg, beaten (you can save the other half for another mug of Cheesecake)

Directions

1. Combine the cream cheese, Greek yogurt, sugar, vanilla extract, and egg in a microwave-safe mug. Beat with a fork until smooth.
2. Microwave on medium-high for 1 min, then stir. Microwave for another minute or until the Cheesecake is set.
3. Let it cool before enjoying. If desired, add your favorite toppings, like fresh fruit or whipped cream.

QUICK FRUIT SALAD

Prep time
5 Min

Cook Time
0 Min

Servings
1

Ingredients

- 1 apple
- 1 banana
- 1 orange
- 1 cup of grapes
- 1 cup of strawberries
- Juice of 1 lemon

Directions

1. Chop all fruits into bite-sized pieces.
2. Combine all fruits in a bowl and toss with lemon juice.
3. Serve immediately or refrigerate before serving.

PEANUT BUTTER BANANA SMOOTHIE

Prep time
5 Min

Cook Time
0 Min

Servings
2

Ingredients

- 2 ripe bananas
- 1 cup milk
- 2 tablespoons peanut butter
- 1 cup ice cubes

Directions

1. Combine all ingredients in a blender.
2. Blend until smooth and creamy.
3. Pour into glasses and serve immediately.

CHOCOLATE AVOCADO MOUSSE

Prep time
5 Min

Cook Time
0 Min

Servings
2

Ingredients

- 1 ripe avocado
- 2 tablespoons cocoa powder
- 2 tablespoons honey or maple syrup
- 1/2 teaspoon vanilla extract

Directions

1. Put everything in a food processor and pulse until combined.
2. Scrape down the edges of the blender as needed and blend until smooth.
3. Divide the mousse between two cups and refrigerate for at least 1 hour before serving.

QUICK APPLE CRISP

Prep time
2 Min

Cook Time
2 Min

Servings
1

Ingredients

- 1 apple, chopped
- 2 tablespoons oats
- 1 tablespoon butter
- 1 tablespoon brown sugar
- 1/4 teaspoon cinnamon

Directions

1. Combine the apple, oats, butter, brown sugar, and cinnamon in a microwave-safe mug.
2. Microwave on high for 2 minutes or until the apple is tender and the topping is crispy.
3. Let it cool for a minute before enjoying it.

MICROWAVE S'MORES

Prep time
1 Min

Cook Time
1 Min

Servings
1

Ingredients

- 1 graham cracker, broken in half
- 1 marshmallow
- 1 piece of chocolate

Directions

1. Place half of the graham cracker on a microwave-safe plate.
2. Top with the piece of chocolate and the marshmallow.
3. Microwave high for 15-20 seconds or until the marshmallow puffs up.
4. Remove from the microwave and top with the other half of the graham cracker. Enjoy!

CREAMY BUTTERNUT SQUASH SOUP

Prep time
5 Min

Cook Time
21 Min

Servings
4

Ingredients

- 1 butternut squash, peeled and chopped
- 1 onion, chopped
- 1 clove of garlic, chopped
- 1/2 cup of cream
- Salt and pepper to taste

Directions

1. Place the butternut squash, onion, and garlic into the soup maker.
2. Set the soup maker to the 'creamy' program. Start the device.
3. Once the soup is cooked, stir in the cream and then add salt & pepper to taste.
4. Serve hot, and if you want, sprinkle with some fresh herbs.

CHUNKY VEGETABLE SOUP

Prep time
5 Min

Cook Time
28 Min

Servings
4

Ingredients

- 1 carrot, chopped
- 1 parsnip, chopped
- 1 onion, chopped
- 2 celery stalks, chopped
- 1 can diced tomatoes
- 4 cups vegetable broth
- Salt and pepper to taste

Directions

1. Add the vegetables, canned tomatoes, and broth into your soup maker.
2. Select the 'chunky' soup setting, and let the machine cycle.
3. Season with salt and pepper and give it a good stir before serving.

SPICY RED LENTIL SOUP

Prep time
5 Min

Cook Time
25 Min

Servings
4

Ingredients

- 1 cup red lentils
- 1 onion, chopped
- 2 cloves garlic, minced
- 1 teaspoon ground cumin
- 1/2 teaspoon chilli powder
- 4 cups vegetable broth
- Salt to taste

Directions

1. Rinse lentils under cold water and add to the soup maker.
2. Add chopped onion, minced garlic, cumin, chilli powder, and vegetable broth.
3. Choose the 'smooth' soup option and let the soup maker do its job.
4. Add salt to taste, and then savor the spicy warmth of your freshly made soup.

CHICKEN NOODLE SOUP

Prep time
5 Min

Cook Time
20 Min

Servings
4

Ingredients

- 2 chicken breasts, diced
- 1 carrot, chopped
- 1 celery stalk, chopped
- 1/2 onion, chopped
- 1/2 cup noodles
- 4 cups chicken broth
- Salt and pepper to taste

Directions

1. Combine chicken, carrot, celery, onion, noodles, and broth in the soup maker.
2. Choose the 'chunky' setting and begin the cooking cycle.
3. Once the cycle is complete, season the soup with salt and pepper and serve hot.

SPINACH AND COCONUT SOUP

Prep time
5 Min

Cook Time
21 Min

Servings
4

Ingredients

- 200g fresh spinach
- 1 onion, chopped
- 1 garlic clove, chopped
- 1 can of coconut milk
- Salt and pepper to taste

Directions

1. Add the spinach, onion, and garlic into the soup maker.
2. Close the lid, select your soup maker's 'smooth' setting, and begin cooking.
3. Once the cooking cycle is complete, open the lid and add the coconut milk to the soup maker.
4. Stir well to combine the coconut milk with the cooked vegetables, ensuring that everything is evenly distributed.
5. Close the lid again and let it blend for a minute or two until everything is smoothly incorporated.
6. Finally, season with salt and pepper as per your taste preference.
7. Stir again, ladle the soup into bowls, and serve hot. For an added touch, garnish with a sprinkle of crushed red pepper flakes or a few fresh spinach leaves. Enjoy this creamy, nourishing Spinach and Coconut Soup!

HEARTY BLACK BEAN SOUP

Prep time
5 Min

Cook Time
25 Min

Servings
4

Ingredients

- 2 cans black beans, drained and rinsed
- 1 onion, chopped
- 1 bell pepper, chopped
- 2 cloves garlic, minced
- 1 tsp ground cumin
- 4 cups vegetable broth
- Salt and pepper to taste

Directions

1. Add the black beans, chopped onion, bell pepper, minced garlic, and cumin to your soup maker.
2. Pour the vegetable broth, and select the 'smooth' setting to start the cooking cycle.
3. Once done, adjust the seasoning with salt and pepper. Ladle the soup into bowls, and serve with a squeeze of lime if desired.

TOMATO AND BASIL SOUP

Prep time
5 Min

Cook Time
20 Min

Servings
4

Ingredients

- 1 can of diced tomatoes
- 1 onion, chopped
- 2 cloves of garlic, chopped
- A handful of fresh basil leaves
- 2 cups vegetable broth
- Salt and pepper to taste

Directions

1. Add the diced tomatoes, chopped onion, garlic, and basil leaves into the soup maker.
2. Pour the vegetable broth, select the 'creamy' option, and start the machine.
3. Taste the soup and adjust the season with salt & pepper when ready. Served warm with a garnish of fresh basil leaves and a drizzle of olive oil.

MUSHROOM SOUP

Prep time
5 Min

Cook Time
20 Min

Servings
4

Ingredients

- 500g mixed mushrooms, chopped
- 1 onion, chopped
- 2 cloves garlic, minced
- 3 cups vegetable broth
- Salt and pepper to taste

Directions

1. Place the chopped mushrooms, onion, and minced garlic into your soup maker.
2. Add the vegetable broth, select the 'smooth' setting, and let the soup maker work magic.
3. Once the cycle is complete, taste and adjust the seasoning with salt and pepper. Served hot, garnished with a sprinkle of fresh parsley and a dollop of cream.

PEA AND MINT SOUP

Prep time
5 Min

Cook Time
20 Min

Servings
4

Ingredients

- 1 bag of frozen peas
- 1 onion, chopped
- 1 garlic clove, chopped
- A handful of fresh mint leaves
- 3 cups vegetable broth
- Salt and pepper to taste

Directions

1. Put the frozen peas, chopped onion, garlic, and fresh mint leaves into the soup maker.
2. Add the vegetable broth and select the 'smooth' setting.
3. After the cooking cycle, season to taste with salt & pepper, and serve the soup hot with a garnish of fresh mint leaves.

SWEET POTATO AND GINGER SOUP

Prep time
5 Min

Cook Time
25 Min

Servings
4

Ingredients

- 2 sweet potatoes, peeled and chopped
- 1 onion, chopped
- 1-inch piece of fresh ginger, minced
- 3 cups vegetable broth
- Salt and pepper to taste

Directions

1. Place the chopped sweet potatoes, onion, and minced ginger into your soup maker.
2. Pour in the vegetable broth over the mixture.
3. Select the 'smooth' setting and allow the soup maker to complete its cycle.
4. Add salt and pepper to taste.
5. Ladle the soup into serving bowls. This soup can be garnished with a drizzle of cream, a sprinkle of chives, or a squeeze of lime juice if desired.

CARROT AND GINGER SOUP

Prep time
5 Min

Cook Time
22 Min

Servings
4

Ingredients

- 4 large carrots, peeled and chopped
- 1 onion, chopped
- 1-inch fresh ginger, peeled and minced
- 3 cups vegetable broth
- Salt and pepper to taste

Directions

1. Load the chopped carrots, onion, and ginger into your soup maker.
2. Pour the vegetable broth, then choose the 'smooth' setting to begin cooking.
3. After the cycle is finished, add salt and pepper to taste. Serve it hot with a swirl of cream and a garnish of chopped parsley.

LENTIL AND VEGETABLE SOUP

Prep time
5 Min

Cook Time
28 Min

Servings
4

Ingredients

- 1 cup dried lentils, rinsed
- 1 carrot, chopped
- 1 celery stalk, chopped
- 1/2 onion, chopped
- 4 cups vegetable broth
- Salt and pepper to taste

Directions

1. Add lentils, chopped carrot, celery, onion, and vegetable broth to the soup maker.
2. Select the 'chunky' setting to begin the cooking cycle.
3. When the cycle is complete, taste and add salt and pepper as needed. Serve heated with a crusty slice of bread.

MINESTRONE SOUP

Prep time
5 Min

Cook Time
25 Min

Servings
4

Ingredients

- 1 can mixed vegetables
- 1/2 cup small pasta
- 1 can diced tomatoes
- 1/2 onion, chopped
- 2 cloves garlic, minced
- 4 cups vegetable broth
- Salt and pepper to taste

Directions

1. Add mixed vegetables, small pasta, diced tomatoes, onion, and garlic to your soup maker.
2. Pour the vegetable broth, and select the 'chunky' soup option to start cooking.
3. Once the soup is ready, season with salt and pepper. Sprinkle with parmesan cheese and serve hot.

PUMPKIN SOUP

Prep time
5 Min

Cook Time
22 Min

Servings
4

Ingredients

- 2 cups pumpkin puree
- 1 onion, chopped
- 1 clove garlic, minced
- 1/2 teaspoon nutmeg
- 3 cups vegetable broth
- Salt and pepper to taste

Directions

1. Add the pumpkin puree, onion, garlic, and nutmeg to the soup maker.
2. Pour the vegetable broth, and select the 'smooth' setting to start the cycle.
3. Once the soup is done, season with salt and pepper to taste. Serve hot, garnished with a dollop of cream.

BEETROOT AND COCONUT SOUP

Prep time
5 Min

Cook Time
25 Min

Servings
4

Ingredients

- 4 medium beetroot, peeled and chopped
- 1 onion, chopped
- 1 clove garlic, minced
- 1 can of coconut milk
- Salt and pepper to taste

Directions

1. Place the chopped beetroots, onion, and minced garlic into your soup maker.
2. Pour in the coconut milk over the vegetables.
3. Close the lid of your soup maker and select the 'smooth' setting. Start the machine and let it cook.
4. Once the soup maker has finished its cycle, open the lid and stir the soup.
5. Taste and adjust the seasoning by putting salt and pepper if necessary.
6. Ladle the soup into bowls, then serve hot. You can garnish with a swirl of coconut milk or a fresh chopped parsley sprinkle. Enjoy your vibrant, creamy, and flavorful Beetroot and Coconut Soup!

ON THE TABLE IN 5 MINUTES

CAPRESE SALAD

Prep time
5 Min

Cook Time
0 Min

Servings
2

Ingredients

- 2 ripe tomatoes
- 1 fresh mozzarella ball
- Fresh basil leaves
- Olive oil
- Balsamic vinegar
- Salt and pepper to taste

Directions

1. Slice the tomatoes and mozzarella into equal slices.
2. Layer the tomato, mozzarella, and basil leaves alternately on a plate.
3. Drizzle with olive oil and balsamic vinegar.
4. Season with salt and pepper to taste. Serve immediately.

CLASSIC CAESAR SALAD

Prep time
5 Min

Cook Time
0 Min

Servings
2

Ingredients

- 1 head of romaine lettuce
- 1/4 cup Caesar salad dressing
- 1/4 cup shredded parmesan cheese
- 1 cup croutons

Directions

1. Rinse and chop the romaine lettuce into bite-sized pieces.
2. In a large-sized bowl, toss the lettuce with Caesar dressing until well-coated.
3. Sprinkle shredded parmesan cheese and croutons on top. Serve immediately.

COUSCOUS SALAD

Prep time
5 Min

Cook Time
2 Min

Servings
4

Ingredients

- 2 cups cooked couscous
- 1 cup cherry tomatoes, halved
- 1 cucumber, diced
- 1/2 cup crumbled feta cheese
- 1/4 cup olive oil
- 2 tablespoons lemon juice
- Salt and pepper to taste

Directions

1. Cook the couscous according to package instructions or cover it with boiling water until it becomes fluffy. Once cooked, fluff it with a fork and let it cool.
2. Combine the cooked couscous, cherry tomatoes, cucumber, and crumbled feta cheese in a large bowl.
3. Mix olive oil, lime juice, salt & pepper in a small-sized bowl to make the dressing.
4. Pour the dressing over the couscous blend and toss until everything is well-coated.
5. Taste and adjust the seasoning if needed.
6. Serve the couscous salad immediately or refrigerate until ready to serve.

GREEK SALAD

Prep time
5 Min

Cook Time
0 Min

Servings
2

Ingredients

- 1 cucumber
- 2 tomatoes
- 1/2 red onion
- 1/2 cup feta cheese
- 1/4 cup olives
- 1/4 cup olive oil
- 1 tablespoon red wine vinegar
- Salt and pepper to taste

Directions

1. Chop the cucumber, tomatoes, and onion into bite-sized pieces.
2. Combine the chopped vegetables, feta cheese, and olives in a large bowl.
3. Whisk the oil, vinegar, salt, and pepper in a small bowl.
4. Drizzle the dressing on the salad and then toss to combine. Serve immediately.

CHICKEN SALAD

Prep time
5 Min

Cook Time
0 Min

Servings
2

Ingredients

- 2 cups cooked chicken, diced
- 1/4 cup mayonnaise
- 2 celery stalks, chopped
- 1/4 cup dried cranberries
- Salt and pepper to taste

Directions

1. Combine the chicken, mayonnaise, chopped celery, and dried cranberries in a large bowl.
2. Mix well until everything is evenly coated with mayonnaise. Season with salt and pepper to taste.
3. Serve the chicken salad on its own, on a bed of lettuce, or as a stuffing for a sandwich.

SHRIMP SALAD

Prep time
5 Min

Cook Time
0 Min

Servings
2

Ingredients

- 2 cups cooked shrimp
- 2 cups mixed greens
- 1/2 cup cherry tomatoes, halved
- 1/4 cup cucumber, diced
- 1/4 cup Italian dressing

Directions

1. Combine the shrimp, mixed greens, cherry tomatoes, and cucumber in a large bowl.
2. Drizzle the salad with Italian dressing. Toss gently to mix. Serve immediately.

TACO SALAD

Prep time
5 Min

Cook Time
0 Min

Servings
2

Ingredients

- 2 cups lettuce, shredded
- 1 cup cooked ground beef or turkey seasoned with taco seasoning
- 1/2 cup shredded cheese
- 1/2 cup salsa
- 1/2 cup tortilla chips, crushed
- 1/4 cup sour cream (optional)

Directions

1. Divide the shredded lettuce between two plates.
2. Top each plate with half the cooked, seasoned meat, shredded cheese, salsa, and crushed tortilla chips.
3. Drizzle with sour cream if desired. Serve immediately.

TUNA PASTA SALAD

Prep time
5 Min

Cook Time
0 Min

Servings
2

Ingredients

- 2 cups cooked pasta
- 1 can of tuna, drained
- 1/2 cup mayonnaise
- 1/4 cup diced celery
- 1/4 cup diced red onion
- Salt and pepper to taste

Directions

1. Combine the cooked pasta, tuna, mayonnaise, celery, and red onion in a large bowl.
2. Stir until everything is well coated with the mayonnaise. Season with salt and pepper to taste.
3. Serve the pasta salad chilled or at room temperature.

TUNA SALAD WRAPS

Prep time
5 Min

Cook Time
0 Min

Servings
4

Ingredients

- 1 can of tuna, drained
- 1/4 cup mayonnaise
- 1/2 celery stalk, finely chopped
- 1/4 onion, finely chopped
- Salt and pepper to taste
- 4 tortilla wraps
- Lettuce leaves

Directions

1. Mix the tuna, mayonnaise, chopped celery, and chopped onion in a bowl. Season with salt and pepper to taste.
2. Lay a tortilla wrap, and place some lettuce leaves in the middle.
3. Spoon some of the tuna mixtures onto the lettuce.
4. Roll the tortilla wrap tightly. Repeat with the remaining wraps.

CHICKEN CAESAR WRAP

Prep time
5 Min

Cook Time
0 Min

Servings
1

Ingredients

- 1 tortilla wrap
- 1/2 cup cooked chicken, sliced
- 1/4 cup Caesar salad dressing
- 1/4 cup shredded romaine lettuce
- 2 tablespoons grated parmesan cheese

Directions

1. Lay the tortilla wrap flat on a plate.
2. Spread the Caesar dressing evenly over the tortilla.
3. Add the chicken slices, shredded lettuce, and parmesan cheese to one side of the tortilla.
4. Roll up the tortilla, tucking in the ends as you go. Cut in half and serve immediately.

BEANS ON TOAST WITH FRIED EGGS

Prep time
5 Min

Cook Time
5 Min

Servings
2

Ingredients

- 4 slices of bread
- 1 can (15 oz) beans (baked beans or your choice)
- 4 eggs
- Butter or cooking oil
- Salt and pepper, to taste
- Optional toppings: grated cheese, chopped parsley

Directions

1. Toast bread until golden brown.
2. Warm beans in microwave or on stovetop.
3. Heat a frying pan, add butter or oil.
4. Crack eggs into the pan, season with salt and pepper.
5. Cook eggs for 2-3 minutes for runny yolks.
6. Spread warm beans on toast slices.
7. Place a fried egg on each slice.
8. Optional: Add grated cheese.
9. Top with chopped parsley if desired.
10. Serve immediately for a quick and tasty meal.

HAM AND EGG BREAKFAST BURRITO

Prep time
3 Min

Cook Time
2 Min

Servings
1

Ingredients

- 1 tortilla
- 1 egg
- 2 slices of ham
- 1/4 cup shredded cheese
- 1 tablespoon salsa

Directions

1. Beat the egg in a microwave-safe bowl, then microwave on high for 1 minute or until fully cooked.
2. Lay the tortilla flat and layer the cooked egg, ham slices, and shredded cheese in the center.
3. Roll up the tortilla, folding in the sides as you go.
4. Microwave the burrito for 15-20 seconds to melt the cheese. Top with salsa and serve.

SALMON AND CREAM CHEESE BAGEL

Prep time
5 Min

Cook Time
0 Min

Servings
1

Ingredients

- 1 bagel, sliced in half
- 2 tablespoons cream cheese
- 2 slices of smoked salmon
- Thinly sliced red onion and capers (optiona

Directions

1. Toast the bagel halves until golden brown.
2. Spread one tablespoon of cream cheese on each half.
3. Lay a slice of smoked salmon over the cream cheese on each half.
4. Top with red onion and capers if desired. Serve immediately.

QUESADILLA

Prep time
3 Min

Cook Time
2 Min

Servings
1

Ingredients

- 2 tortillas
- 1/2 cup shredded cheese (cheddar, mozzarella, or a mix)
- 1/4 cup diced cooked chicken (optional)
- Salsa, sour cream, or guacamole for serving

Directions

1. Lay one tortilla on a plate and sprinkle half the cheese.
2. If using, spread the cooked chicken evenly over the cheese.
3. Sprinkle the rest of the cheese on top, then cover with the second tortilla.
4. Warm a non-stick skillet over moderate heat and transfer the quesadilla to the skillet.
5. Cook until the bottom tortilla is golden brown, then flip and cook until the other side gets golden and the cheese is melted.
6. Slice into quarters and serve hot with salsa, sour cream, or guacamole.

GREEK PITA

Prep time
5 Min

Cook Time
0 Min

Servings
2

Ingredients

- 2 pita bread
- 1/2 cup cooked chicken, sliced
- 1/2 cup cucumber, diced
- 1/4 cup feta cheese
- 1/4 cup olives, sliced
- 2 tablespoons Greek dressing

Directions

1. Warm up the pita bread in the microwave for 10-15 seconds.
2. Open each pita bread to form a pocket.
3. Add half the chicken, cucumber, feta cheese, and olives to each pocket.
4. Drizzle each with Greek dressing. Serve immediately.

PITA PIZZAS

Prep time
2 Min

Cook Time
3 Min

Servings
2

Ingredients

- 2 pita bread
- 1/2 cup pizza sauce
- 1/2 cup shredded mozzarella cheese
- Toppings of your choice (pepperoni, mushrooms, bell peppers, etc.)

Directions

1. Set your oven's temperature or toaster oven to 350°F (175°C).
2. Spread pizza sauce over each pita bread.
3. Sprinkle shredded mozzarella over the sauce.
4. Add your desired toppings.
5. Bake in the oven for 3 mins or until the cheese gets melted and slightly golden. Be careful not to burn the pita.

AVOCADO TOAST

Prep time
3 Min

Cook Time
2 Min

Servings
2

Ingredients

- 1 ripe avocado
- 2 slices of bread
- Lemon juice
- Salt and pepper to taste

Directions

1. Toast the bread slices until they get golden brown.
2. Cut the avocado in half and remove the seed before scooping the flesh into a bowl.
3. Mash the avocado with a fork and add a few drops of lemon juice.
4. Season with salt and pepper.
5. Place the avocado mixture on the toasted bread. Serve immediately.

TUNA NICOISE SALAD

Prep time
10 Min

Cook Time
0 Min

Servings
1

Ingredients

- 2 cups mixed salad greens
- 1 can tuna, drained
- 1/4 cup cherry tomatoes, halved
- 1/4 cup sliced cucumber
- 2 tablespoons sliced black olives
- 1 hard-boiled egg, sliced
- 1/4 cup blanched green beans
- 2 tablespoons red onion, thinly sliced
- 2 tablespoons extra-virgin olive oil
- 1 tablespoon red wine vinegar
- Salt and pepper to taste
- Fresh parsley for garnish

Directions

1. Arrange the mixed salad greens as the base in a large salad bowl.
2. Top with drained tuna, cherry tomatoes, sliced cucumber, black olives, hard-boiled egg, blanched green beans, and thinly sliced red onion.
3. Drizzle with extra-virgin olive oil and red wine vinegar.
4. Season with salt and pepper to taste.
5. Gently toss all the ingredients together until well combined.
6. Garnish the salad with fresh parsley.
7. Serve the Tuna Niçoise Salad immediately as a satisfying and nutritious meal.

CHEESY GARLIC BREAD

Prep time
3 Min

Cook Time
2 Min

Servings
4

Ingredients

- 4 slices of bread
- 2 tablespoons softened butter
- 2 garlic cloves, minced
- 1 cup shredded mozzarella cheese

Directions

1. Warm your oven or toaster oven to 350°F (175°C).
2. In a small-sized bowl, mix the softened butter with minced garlic.
3. Spread the garlic butter over one side of each slice of bread.
4. Sprinkle the shredded mozzarella over the buttered side of the bread.
5. Bake in the oven for 2 minutes or until the cheese is melted and bubbly. Serve hot.

BLT SANDWICH

Prep time
5 Min

Cook Time
0 Min

Servings
1

Ingredients

- 2 slices of bread
- 2 lettuce leaves
- 2 slices of tomato
- 2 slices of bacon
- 1 tablespoon mayonnaise

Directions

1. Microwave the bacon for 2 minutes
2. Place the mayonnaise on one side of each slice of bread.
3. Layer the lettuce leaves, tomato slices, and bacon on one piece of bread.
4. Top with the second slice of bread, mayonnaise-side down. Cut in half, if desired, and serve.

HAM AND CHEESE SLIDERS

Prep time
3 Min

Cook Time
2 Min

Servings
4

Ingredients

- 4 mini buns or dinner rolls
- 4 slices of ham
- 4 slices of cheese
- 1 tablespoon mustard
- 1 tablespoon mayonnaise

Directions

1. Cut the buns or rolls in half horizontally.
2. Spread mustard on each bun and mayonnaise on the other half.
3. On the mustard half, place a slice of ham and a slice of cheese.
4. Top with the other half of the bun. Repeat with the remaining buns.
5. Microwave the sliders for 20-30 seconds until the cheese is melted. Serve hot.

TUNA MELT

Prep time
3 Min

Cook Time
2 Min

Servings
1

Ingredients

- 2 slices of bread
- 1 can of tuna, drained
- 2 tablespoons mayonnaise
- 1 slice of cheese
- Salt and pepper to taste

Directions

1. In a small bowl, mix the tuna with mayonnaise. Season with salt and pepper.
2. Place the tuna mixture on one slice of bread and drizzle with a slice of cheese.
3. Cover with the second slice of bread. Cook in a sandwich maker or microwave until the cheese is melted.

PESTO AND SUN-DRIED TOMATO PASTA

Prep time
2 Min

Cook Time
3 Min

Servings
1

Ingredients

- 1 cup cooked pasta of your choice
- 2 tablespoons store-bought pesto sauce
- 2 tablespoons sun-dried tomatoes, chopped
- Grated Parmesan cheese, for garnish (optional)

Directions

1. Combine the cooked pasta, pesto sauce, and chopped sun-dried tomatoes in a bowl.
2. Toss well until the pasta is well coated with the pesto sauce and the sun-dried tomatoes are distributed throughout.
3. If needed, sprinkle grated Parmesan cheese over the top for added flavor.
4. Serve the Pesto and Sun-Dried Tomato Pasta immediately as a quick and delicious meal.

GUACAMOLE WITH CHIPS

Prep time
5 Min

Cook Time
0 Min

Servings
2

Ingredients

- 2 ripe avocados
- 1/2 onion, finely chopped
- 1 tomato, finely chopped
- 1/2 jalapeno, finely chopped (optional)
- 1 lime, juiced
- Salt to taste
- Tortilla chips

Directions

1. Cut the avocados in half, remove the pits, and transfer the flesh to a bowl.
2. Mash the avocado flesh using a fork until it reaches your desired consistency.
3. Mix in the chopped onion, tomato, and jalapeno (if using).
4. Stir in the lime juice and salt. Adjust to taste.
5. Serve immediately with tortilla chips for dipping.

TURKEY ROLL-UPS

Prep time
5 Min

Cook Time
0 Min

Servings
1

Ingredients

- 2 slices of turkey
- 1 tablespoon cream cheese
- 2 slices of cucumber
- 2 lettuce leaves

Directions

1. Place cream cheese on each slice of turkey.
2. Place a lettuce leaf and a slice of cucumber on one end of each slice.
3. Roll the turkey slice starting from the end with the cucumber and lettuce.
4. Secure with a toothpick if necessary. Serve immediately.

VEGETABLE STIR-FRY

Prep time
5 Min

Cook Time
5 Min

Servings
2

Ingredients

- 2 cups mixed vegetables (bell peppers, broccoli, snap peas)
- 1 tablespoon vegetable oil
- 2 tablespoons soy sauce
- 1 teaspoon garlic powder

Directions

1. Warm vegetable oil in a large-sized pan over medium-high heat.
2. Put the mixed vegetables in the pan and cook for 3-4 minutes, stirring frequently.
3. Add the soy sauce and garlic powder. Stir to coat the vegetables.
4. Continue to cook for 1 more minute. Serve hot.

VEGETABLE FRIED RICE

Prep time
3 Min

Cook Time
2 Min

Servings
2

Ingredients

- 2 cups cooked rice
- 1 cup frozen mixed vegetables
- 2 tablespoons soy sauce
- 1 tablespoon vegetable oil

Directions

1. Warm the vegetable oil in a large pan over medium heat.
2. Add the frozen vegetables and heat for 1-2 minutes
3. Add the prepared rice to the pan and stir to combine.
4. Pour the soy sauce over the rice and vegetables, stirring until everything is well mixed. Serve hot.

SPICY GARLIC PASTA

Prep time
2 Min

Cook Time
3 Min

Servings
1

Ingredients

- 1 cup cooked pasta (any variety)
- 1 tablespoon olive oil
- 1 garlic clove, minced
- 1/4 teaspoon red pepper flakes
- Salt and pepper to taste
- Grated Parmesan cheese for garnish
- Chopped fresh parsley for garnish (optional)

Directions

1. Warm the olive oil over moderate heat in a pan.
2. Add mashed garlic and red pepper flakes to the skillet. Sauté until aromatic and golden, about 1 minute.
3. Drain and then add the pasta to the skillet with the garlic-infused oil.
4. Toss pasta in oil to coat. Salt & pepper to taste.
5. Put the pasta in a bowl or on a plate to serve.
6. If desired, sprinkle Parmesan cheese and chopped parsley.
7. Serve immediately.

INSTANT RAMEN STIR-FRY

Prep time
2 Min

Cook Time
3 Min

Servings
2

Ingredients

- 2 packs of instant ramen (flavor packets discarded)
- 1 cup frozen mixed vegetables
- 2 tablespoons soy sauce
- 2 tablespoons vegetable oil

Directions

1. Prepare the ramen noodles per the instructions without adding the flavor packet. Drain and set aside.
2. Warm the vegetable oil in a large pan or wok over medium heat.
3. Add the frozen mixed vegetables and then cook until heated through.
4. Add the cooked ramen noodles to the pan, along with the soy sauce. Stir well to combine. Serve immediately.

SCRAMBLED EGGS WITH CHEESE

Prep time
2 Min

Cook Time
3 Min

Servings
1

Ingredients

- 2 eggs
- 1/4 cup shredded cheddar cheese
- Salt and pepper to taste

Directions

1. In a small-size bowl, beat the eggs and season them with salt and pepper.
2. Set a non-stick skillet on the stove over moderate heat.
3. Pour the beaten eggs into the skillet.
4. Constantly stir the eggs until they start to set.
5. Sprinkle the shredded cheese over the eggs.
6. Continue stirring until the eggs get fully cooked, and the cheese is melted. Serve hot.

HOMEMADE HOUMOUS

Prep time
5 Min

Cook Time
0 Min

Servings
2

Ingredients

- 1 (15-ounce) can chickpeas
- 1/4 cup (60 ml) fresh lemon juice,m
- 1/4 cup (60 ml) well-stirred tahini
- 1 small garlic clove, minced
- 2 tablespoons (30 ml) extra-virgin olive oil, plus more for serving
- 1/2 teaspoon ground cumin
- Salt to taste
- 2 to 3 tablespoons (30 to 45 ml) water or aquafaba,
- Dash ground paprika or sumac, for serving

Directions

1. Blend all the ingredients together until smooth.
2. Serve with your choice of chopped vegetables such as bell pepper, cucumber, carrot, cauliflower and radish.

NACHOS

Prep time
3 Min

Cook Time
2 Min

Servings
2-3

Ingredients

- 1 bag of tortilla chips
- 1 cup shredded cheese (cheddar or Mexican blend)
- 1/2 cup black beans, washed & drained
- 1/2 cup pico de gallo
- 1/4 cup jalapenos (optional)

Directions

1. Set your oven's heat to 350°F (175°C).
2. Place tortilla chips in one layer on a baking sheet.
3. Sprinkle shredded cheese evenly over the chips.
4. Scatter black beans on top.
5. Prepare for 2-3 mins or until cheese is melted.
6. Remove from the oven and immediately top with pico de gallo and jalapenos. Serve hot.

HAM AND CHEESE OMELETTE

Prep time
5 Min

Cook Time
5 Min

Servings
1

Ingredients

- 2 large eggs
- 2 slices of ham, diced
- 1/4 cup shredded cheese (e.g., cheddar, Swiss, or your favorite cheese)
- Salt and pepper to taste
- 1 tablespoon butter

Directions

1. Begin by cracking the eggs into a bowl and whisking them thoroughly until well beaten. Season with salt and pepper.
2. Warm the butter in a non-stick skillet over medium heat until melted and sizzling.
3. Transfer the whisked eggs to the frying pan and let them cook undisturbed for a minute until the edges start to set.
4. Sprinkle the diced ham and shredded cheese evenly over one side of the omelet.
5. Use a spatula to fold the other half of the omelet over the filling to form a half-moon shape.
6. Let the omelet cook for another minute or until the cheese is melted and the eggs are fully cooked.
7. Carefully transfer the omelet to a plate and serve it hot.

BEAN BURRITOS

Prep time
5 Min

Cook Time
0 Min

Servings
4

Ingredients

- 4 tortillas
- 1 can of refried beans
- 1 cup shredded cheddar cheese
- 1/2 cup salsa
- 1/2 cup shredded lettuce

Directions

1. Warm up the tortillas in the microwave for 10-15 seconds.
2. Spread a quarter of the refried beans down the center of each tortilla.
3. Sprinkle a quarter of the shredded cheese over the beans.
4. Top with a spoonful of salsa and some shredded lettuce.
5. Roll up the tortilla, folding in the sides as you go. Repeat with the remaining tortillas. Serve immediately.

MICROWAVE MAC AND CHEESE

Prep time
1 Min

Cook Time
5 Min

Servings
1

Ingredients

- 1/2 cup macaroni
- 1/2 cup water
- 1/2 cup shredded cheddar cheese
- 1/4 cup milk

Directions

1. In a microwave-safe bowl, mix the macaroni and water.
2. Microwave the mixture on high for 2 minutes, then stir.
3. Repeat step 2. The pasta should be cooked, and water should be mostly absorbed.
4. Add the cheese and milk to the pasta. Stir to combine.
5. Microwave the mixture for another 30 to 1 min until the cheese melts. Stir well before serving.

SPAGHETTI AGLIO E OLIO

Prep time
5 Min

Cook Time
0 Min

Servings
2

Ingredients

- 2 servings of fresh spaghetti
- 4 tablespoons olive oil
- 2 garlic cloves, minced
- 1 teaspoon red pepper flakes
- Salt to taste
- Grated Parmesan and chopped parsley for serving

Directions

1. In a large-sized pan, heat the olive oil over medium heat.
2. Add the mashed garlic & red pepper flakes, cooking until the garlic gets fragrant but not browned.
3. Flash boil the spaghetti for 90 seconds then add to the pan and toss until it's coated with the oil and garlic. Season with salt to taste.
4. Serve the spaghetti topped with grated Parmesan and chopped parsley.

SPAGHETTI PUTTANESCA WITH FRESH PASTA

Prep time
5

Cook Time
5 Min

Servings
1

Ingredients

- 1 serving of fresh spaghetti (approximately 2 ounces)
- 2 tablespoons extra-virgin olive oil
- 2 cloves garlic, minced
- 1/4 teaspoon red pepper flakes
- 1/4 cup pitted black olives, sliced
- 2 tablespoons capers
- 1/2 cup canned diced tomatoes
- Salt and pepper to taste
- Fresh parsley, chopped, for garnish

Directions

1. Take a pot of salted water to a boil and cook the fresh spaghetti according to the package instructions until al dente. Drain and set aside.
2. In a large-sized skillet, heat the olive oil over medium heat. Add the mashed garlic and red pepper flakes. Sauté for about 1 minute until the garlic becomes fragrant.
3. Add the sliced black olives and capers to the skillet, and cook for another minute.
4. Stir in the canned diced tomatoes, season with salt & pepper to taste, and allow the sauce simmer for 2-3 minutes.
5. Add the cooked fresh spaghetti to the skillet, and toss well to coat the pasta with the sauce.
6. Cook for one more minute to allow the flavors to meld together.
7. Transfer the Spaghetti Puttanesca to a serving plate or bowl.
8. Garnish with freshly chopped parsley.
9. Serve the Spaghetti Puttanesca immediately, and enjoy the bold flavors of this classic Italian pasta dish.

PESTO PASTA

Prep time
3 Min

Cook Time
2 Min

Servings
2

Ingredients

- 2 servings of fresh pasta
- 1/4 cup pesto sauce
- Grated Parmesan cheese for serving

Pesto Sauce Ingredients

- 2 cups fresh basil leaves
- 1/3 cup grated Parmesan cheese
- 1/4 cup pine nuts
- 2 cloves garlic, minced
- 1/3 cup extra-virgin olive oil
- Salt and pepper to taste

Directions

1. To make the pesto sauce, combine the fresh basil leaves, grated Parmesan cheese, pine nuts, minced garlic, and a pinch of salt and pepper in a food processor or blender.
2. While the food processor is running, slowly drizzle in the extra-virgin olive oil until the mixture is well blended and forms a smooth sauce. Taste and adjust the seasoning if needed.
3. Bring a pot of salted water to a boil and cook the fresh pasta according to the package instructions, usually for about 2 minutes or until al dente.
4. Drain the cooked pasta and transfer it to a large mixing bowl. Add the pesto sauce to the cooked pasta and toss until the pasta is well coated with the sauce.
5. Serve the Pesto Pasta in individual plates or bowls.
6. Sprinkle grated Parmesan cheese on top for added flavor.
7. Enjoy this quick and delicious Pesto Pasta that showcases the vibrant flavors of fresh basil, Parmesan cheese, and pine nuts.

TOMATO AND MOZZARELLA PANINI

Prep time
5 Min

Cook Time
5 Min

Servings
1

Ingredients

- 2 slices of sourdough bread
- 2 slices of fresh mozzarella cheese
- 2-3 slices of tomato
- Fresh basil leaves
- 1 tablespoon of balsamic glaze
- Salt and pepper to taste
- Olive oil for grilling

Directions

1. Preheat a panini press or grill pan.
2. Brush one side of every bread slice with olive oil.
3. Lay one slice of bread, oiled side down, on a clean surface.
4. Layer the mozzarella cheese, tomato slices, and fresh basil leaves on top of the bread.
5. Drizzle the balsamic glaze over the filling. Season with salt and pepper to taste.
6. Place the second slice of bread on top, oiled side up.
7. Transfer the sandwich to the preheated panini press or grill pan.
8. Cook for about 3-4 minutes, or until the bread gets golden brown and crispy, and the cheese has melted.
9. Remove the panini from the press or grill pan and let it cool slightly before slicing in half.

SPEEDY CHEESE AND TOMATO TOASTIES

Prep time
2 Min

Cook Time
3 Min

Servings
1

Ingredients

- 2 slices of bread
- 1/2 cup shredded cheddar cheese
- 1 small tomato, sliced
- Butter or margarine

Directions

1. Place the slices of bread on a clean surface.
2. Spread a thin layer of butter or margarine on one side of each slice.
3. On the non-buttered side of one slice, evenly distribute the shredded cheddar cheese. Layer the sliced tomatoes on top of the cheese.
4. Place the second slice of bread on top, buttered side facing out.
5. Preheat a non-stick skillet or sandwich press over medium heat.
6. Carefully transfer the assembled sandwich to the skillet or sandwich press.
7. Cook for about 1-2 minutes on each side, or until the bread is golden brown and the cheese is melted.
8. Remove from the heat and let it cool for a moment before slicing.
9. Serve your speedy cheese and tomato toastie while warm and gooey.

Printed in Great Britain
by Amazon

33798052R00064